PIANO • VOCAL • GUITAR

ꓥꓤꓰ OF THE FIFTIES

T H E   D E C A D E   S E R I E S

D0770854

ISBN 0-7935-3094-6

HAL•LEONARD
CORPORATION
7777 W. BLUEMOUND RD. P.O. BOX 13819 MILWAUKEE, WI 53213

MORE SONGS OF THE FIFTIES
THE DECADE SERIES

CONTENTS

ALL OF YOU
(From "SILK STOCKINGS")

Words and Music by
COLE PORTER

Fox trot tempo

After watch-ing her ap-peal from ev-'ry an-gle, there's a big ro-man-tic deal I've got to wan-gle. For I've fal-len for a

ALL THE WAY
(From "THE JOKER IS WILD")

Words by SAMMY CAHN
Music by JAMES VAN HEUSEN

When some-bod-y loves you, it's no good un-less he loves you all the way.
When some-bod-y needs you, it's no good un-less she needs you all the way.

Hap-py to be near you, when you need some-one to cheer you all the way.
Thru the good or lean years and for all the in be-tween years, come what may.

Tall-er than the tall-est tree is,
Who knows where the road will lead us,

ALLEGHENY MOON

Words and Music by DICK MANNING
and AL HOFFMAN

ALRIGHT, OKAY, YOU WIN

Words and Music by SID WYCHE
and MAYME WATTS

Moderately, with rhythm

BABY
(YOU'VE GOT WHAT IT TAKES)

Words and Music by CLYDE OTIS
and MURRAY STEIN

THE BALLAD OF DAVY CROCKETT

(From "DAVY CROCKETT, KING OF THE WILD FRONTIER")

Words by TOM BLACKBURN
Music by GEORGE BRUNS

VERSES

4.
Andy Jackson is our gen'ral's name,
His reg'lar soldiers we'll put to shame,
Them redskin varmints us Volunteers'll tame,
'Cause we got the guns with the sure-fire aim.
Davy — Davy Crockett,
The champion of us all!

5.
Headed back to war from the ol' home place,
But Red Stick was leadin' a merry chase,
Fightin' an' burnin' at a devil's pace
South to the swamps on the Florida Trace.
Davy — Davy Crockett,
Trackin' the redskins down!

6.
Fought single-handed through the Injun War
Till the Creeks was whipped an' peace was in store,
An' while he was handlin' this risky chore,
Made hisself a legend for evermore.
Davy — Davy Crockett,
King of the wild frontier!

7.
He give his word an' he give his hand
That his Injun friends could keep their land,
An' the rest of his life he took the stand
That justice was due every redskin band.
Davy — Davy Crockett,
Holdin' his promise dear!

8.
Home fer the winter with his family,
Happy as squirrels in the ol' gum tree,
Bein' the father he wanted to be,
Close to his boys as the pod an' the pea.
Davy — Davy Crockett,
Holdin' his young 'uns dear!

9.
But the ice went out an' the warm winds came
An' the meltin' snow showed tracks of game,
An' the flowers of Spring filled the woods with flame,
An' all of a sudden life got too tame.
Davy — Davy Crockett,
Headin' on West again!

10.
Off through the woods we're riding' along,
Makin' up yarns an' singin' a song,
He's ringy as a b'ar an' twict as strong,
An' knows he's right 'cause he ain't often wrong.
Davy — Davy Crockett,
The man who don't know fear!

11.
Lookin' fer a place where the air smells clean,
Where the trees is tall an' the grass is green,
Where the fish is fat in an untouched stream,
An' the teemin' woods is a hunter's dream.
Davy — Davy Crockett,
Lookin' fer Paradise!

12.
Now he'd lost his love an' his grief was gall,
In his heart he wanted to leave it all,
An' lose himself in the forests tall,
But he answered instead his country's call.
Davy — Davy Crockett,
Beginnin' his campaign!

13.
Needin' his help they didn't vote blind,
They put in Davy 'cause he was their kind,
Sent up to Nashville the best they could find,
A fightin' spirit an' a thinkin' mind.
Davy — Davy Crockett,
Choice of the whole frontier!

14.
The votes were counted an' he won hands down,
So they sent him off to Washin'ton town
With his best dress suit still his buckskins brown,
A livin' legend of growin' renown.
Davy — Davy Crockett,
The Canebrake Congressman!

15.
He went off to Congress an' served a spell,
Fixin' up the Gover'ment an' laws as well,
Took over Washin'ton so we heered tell
An' patched up the crack in the Liberty Bell.
Davy — Davy Crockett,
Seein' his duty clear!

16.
Him an' his jokes travelled all through the land,
An' his speeches made him friends to beat the band,
His politickin' was their favorite brand
An' everyone wanted to shake his hand.
Davy — Davy Crockett,
Helpin' his legend grow!

17.
He knew when he spoke he sounded the knell
Of his hopes for White House an' fame as well,
But he spoke out strong so hist'ry books tell
An patched up the crack in the Liberty Bell.
Davy — Davy Crockett,
Seein' his duty clear!

BIRD DOG

By BOUDLEAUX BRYANT

VERSE 2. Johnny sings a love song *(Like a bird)*
He sings the sweetest love song *(You ever heard)*
But when he sings to my gal *(What a howl)*
To me he's just a wolf dog *(On the prowl)*
Johnny wants to fly away and puppy love my baby *(He's a bird dog)*
(CHORUS)

3. Johnny kissed the teacher *(He's a bird)*
He tiptoed up to reach her *(He's a bird)*
Well, he's the teacher's pet now *(He's a dog)*
What he wants he can get now *(What a dog)*
He even made the teacher let him sit next to my baby. *(He's a bird dog)*
(CHORUS)

THE BIBLE TELLS ME SO

Words and Music by
DALE EVANS

BYE BYE LOVE

Words and Music by FELICE BRYANT
and BOUDLEAUX BRYANT

Moderately fast

BLUEBERRY HILL

Words and Music by AL LEWIS,
LARRY STOCK and VINCENT ROSE

CHARLIE BROWN

Words and Music by JERRY LEIBER
and MIKE STOLLER

CHANSON D'AMOUR
(THE RA-DA-DA-DA-DA SONG)

Words and Music by
WAYNE SHANKLIN

THE CHIPMUNK SONG

Words and Music by
ROSS BAGDASARIAN

DO I LOVE YOU BECAUSE YOU'RE BEAUTIFUL?

(From "CINDERELLA")

Lyrics by OSCAR HAMMERSTEIN II
Music by RICHARD RODGERS

DO-RE-MI
(From "THE SOUND OF MUSIC")

Lyrics by OSCAR HAMMERSTEIN II
Music by RICHARD RODGERS

DOMINO

English Words by DON RAYE
French Words by JACQUES PLANTE
Music by LOUIS FERRARI

MCA music publishing

FLY ME TO THE MOON
(IN OTHER WORDS)

Words and Music by
BART HOWARD

Bossa Nova

Cm7

Fly me to the moon, and let me play a - mong the stars;

Fm7 **Bb7**

Ebmaj7 **Ab** **Dm7-5**

Let me see what spring is like on

G7-9 **Cm** **C7** **Fm7** **Ab/Bb**

Ju - pi - ter and Mars. In oth - er words,

FROM THIS MOMENT ON
(From "OUT OF THIS WORLD")

Words and Music by
COLE PORTER

Lyrics:
Now that we are close, no more nights mor-ose, Now that we are one, the be-guine has just be-gun. Now that we're side by side, the fu-ture looks so gay, Now we are

mo - ment on. From this hap - py day,

no more blue

songs, on - ly whoop - dee - doo songs,

from this mo - ment on. For you've got the love

HAPPY, HAPPY BIRTHDAY BABY

Words and Music by MARGO SYLVIA
and GILBERT LOPEZ

HELLO, YOUNG LOVERS
(From "THE KING AND I")

Lyrics by OSCAR HAMMERSTEIN II
Music by RICHARD RODGERS

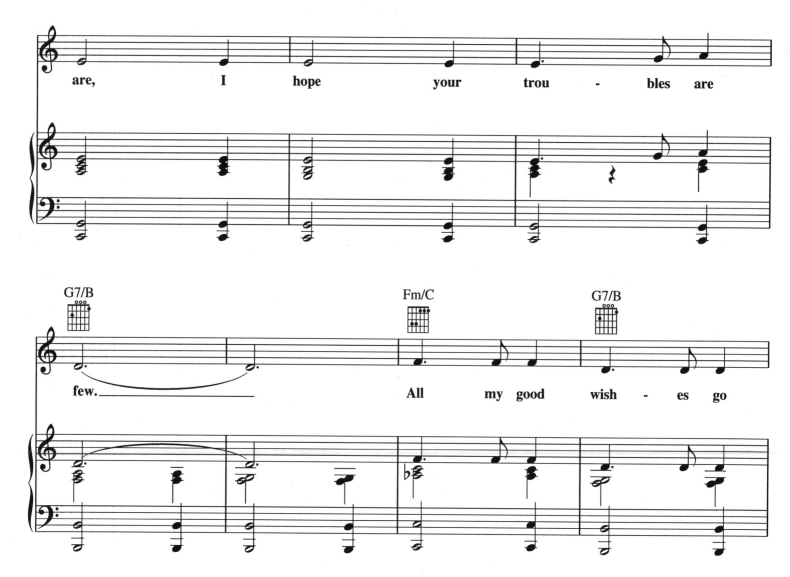

with you to-night. I've been in love like you _____ Be brave, young lov-ers, and fol-low your star; be brave and faith-ful and true. _____ Cling ver-y close to each

HEY, GOOD LOOKIN'

Words and Music by
HANK WILLIAMS

Moderately

HOUND DOG

Words and Music by JERRY LEIBER
and MIKE STOLLER

Medium Rock

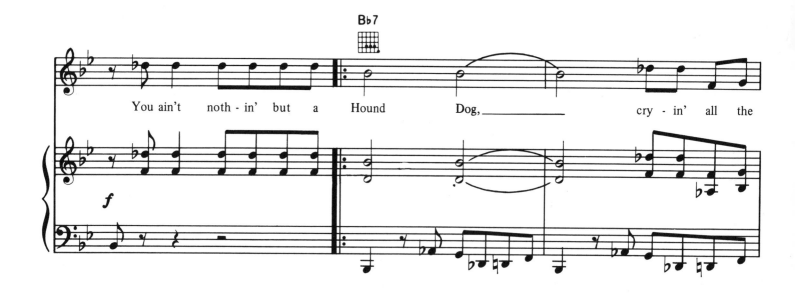

You ain't noth-in' but a Hound Dog,_____ cry-in' all the

time. You ain't noth-in' but a Hound Dog,_____

I AM IN LOVE

Words and Music by
COLE PORTER

Sit down, if you please and from laugh-ing re-frain, Sit down, if you please, and I beg you try to lis-ten while I ex-plain:

REFRAIN (Moderate, steady fox-trot)

I am de-ject-ed, I am de-pressed,

I COULD HAVE DANCED ALL NIGHT

(From "MY FAIR LADY")

Words by ALAN JAY LERNER
Music by FREDERICK LOEWE

I LEFT MY HEART IN SAN FRANCISCO

Words by DOUGLAS CROSS
Music by GEORGE CORY

With a slow, steady beat

I WANNA BE LOVED

Words by BILLY ROSE and EDWARD HEYMAN
Music by JOHNNY GREEN

I WHISTLE A HAPPY TUNE
(From "THE KING AND I")

Lyrics by OSCAR HAMMERSTEIN II
Music by RICHARD RODGERS

shoes I strike a care-less pose And whis-tle a hap-py tune And no-one ev-er knows I'm a-fraid _____ The re-sult of this de-cep-tion is ver-y strange to_ tell For when I fool the peo-ple I fear, I

I'VE GROWN ACCUSTOMED TO HER FACE

(From "MY FAIR LADY")

Words by ALAN JAY LERNER
Music by FREDERICK LOEWE

IT'S ALL RIGHT WITH ME

(From "CAN-CAN")

Words and Music by
COLE PORTER

LONG BEFORE I KNEW YOU

(From "BELLS ARE RINGING")

Words by BETTY COMDEN and ADOLPH GREEN
Music by JULE STYNE

KISS OF FIRE

Words and Music by LESTER ALLEN
and ROBERT HILL
(Adapted from A.G. VILLOLDO)

Moderate Tango

I touch your lips and all at once the sparks go fly-ing. Those dev-il

lips that know so well the art of ly-ing. And tho' I see the dan-ger, still the flame grows

LAZY AFTERNOON

Words by JOHN LATOUCHE
Music by JEROME MOROSS

LOVE AND MARRIAGE

Words by SAMMY CAHN
Music by JAMES VAN HEUSEN

Schottische tempo

LOVE AND MAR - RIAGE, LOVE AND MAR - RIAGE,

Go to-geth - er like a horse and car - riage, This I tell ya

It's an in - sti - tute you can't dis - par - age, ask the lo - cal

LOVE, LOOK AWAY
(From "FLOWER DRUM SONG")

Lyrics by OSCAR HAMMERSTEIN II
Music by RICHARD RODGERS

MACK THE KNIFE

English Words by MARC BLITZSTEIN
Original German Words by BERT BRECHT
Music by KURT WEILL

MAGIC MOMENTS

Lyric by HAL DAVID
Music by BURT BACHARACH

1. I'll nev-er for-get the mo-ment we kissed the night of the hay - ride,
2. The tel - e -phone call that tied up the line for hours— and hours,_____
3. The way that we cheered when-ev - er our team was scor-ing a touch - down,
4. The pen - ny ar - cade, the games that we played, the fun and the priz - es,

the way that we hugged to try to keep warm while tak-ing a sleigh - ride;

the Sat - ur - day dance {I / you} got up the nerve to send {you / me} some flow - ers;

the time that the floor fell out of {my / your} car when {I / you} put the clutch down;

the Hal - low - een Hop when ev - 'ry -one came in fun - ny dis - guis - es;

MONA LISA
(From The Paramount Picture "CAPTAIN CAREY, U.S.A.")

Words and Music by JAY LIVINGSTON
and RAY EVANS

MY FAVORITE THINGS
(From "THE SOUND OF MUSIC")

Lyrics by OSCAR HAMMERSTEIN II
Music by RICHARD RODGERS

P.S. I LOVE YOU

Words by JOHNNY MERCER
Music by GORDON JENKINS

MCA music publishing

(You'VE GOT)
PERSONALITY

Words and Music by HAROLD LOGAN
and LLOYD PRICE

SECRET LOVE

Lyrics by PAUL FRANCIS WEBSTER
Music by SAMMY FAIN

SHRIMP BOATS

Words and Music by PAUL HOWARD
and PAUL WESTON

Shrimp boats is a-com-in', Their sails are in sight.

Shrimp boats is a-com-in', There's danc-in' to-night. Why don't-cha

Shrimp boats is a-com-in', There's danc-in' to-

night. Why don't-cha hur-ry, hur-ry, hur-ry home, Why don't-cha

hur-ry, hur-ry, hur-ry home? *(look here the)* Shrimp boats is a-

com-in', There's danc-in' to-night. night.

SIXTEEN TONS

Words and Music by
MERLE TRAVIS

SMALL WORLD
(From "GYPSY")

Words by STEPHEN SONDHEIM
Music by JULE STYNE

(LET ME BE YOUR)
TEDDY BEAR

Words and Music by KAL MANN
and BERNIE LOWE

Medium Bright Rock

Chorus

1. Ba - by, let me be your lov - in' Ted - dy
2. Ba - by, let me be a - round you ev - 'ry

Bear.
night.

Put a chain a - round my neck ____ and
Run your fin - gers round through my hair ____ and

THAT'S AMORE
(THAT'S LOVE)
(From The Paramount Picture "THE CADDY")

Words by JACK BROOKS
Music by HARRY WARREN

TILL

Words by CARL SIGMAN
Music by CHARLES DANVERS

THAT'S ENTERTAINMENT
(From "THE BAND WAGON")

Words by HOWARD DIETZ
Music by ARTHUR SCHWARTZ

TUTTI FRUTTI

Words and Music by RICHARD PENNIMAN
and D. LA BOSTRIE

MCA music publishing

TOO MUCH

Words and Music by LEE ROSENBERG
and BERNIE WEINMAN

WHY

Words and Music by BOB MARCUCCI
and PETER DeANGELIS

MCA music publishing

WISH YOU WERE HERE

(From "WISH YOU WERE HERE")

Words and Music by
HAROLD ROME

YOUR CHEATIN' HEART

Words and Music by
HANK WILLIAMS

YAKETY YAK

Words and Music by JERRY LEIBER
and MIKE STOLLER

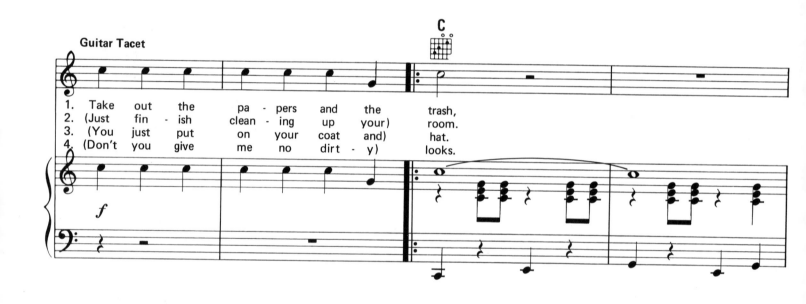

(I WONDER WHY?)
YOU'RE JUST IN LOVE
(From The Stage Production "CALL ME MADAM")

Words and Music by
IRVING BERLIN

YOUNG AND FOOLISH
(From "PLAIN AND FANCY")

Words by ARNOLD B. HORWITT
Music by ALBERT HAGUE

THE DECADE SERIES

The Decade Series explores the music of the 1890's to the 1980's through each era's major events and personalities. Each volume features text and photos and over 40 of the decade's top songs, so readers can see how music has acted as a mirror or a catalyst for current events and trends. Each book is arranged for piano, voice & guitar.

Songs Of The 1890's
Over 50 songs, including: America, The Beautiful • The Band Played On • Hello! Ma Baby • Maple Leaf Rag • My Wild Irish Rose • O Sole Mio • The Sidewalks Of New York • The Stars And Stripes Forever • Ta Ra Ra Boom De Ay • Who Threw The Overalls In Mistress Murphy's Chowder • and more.
_____00311655 ....$12.95

Songs Of The 1900s – 1900-1909
Over 50 favorites, including: Anchors Aweigh • Bill Bailey, Won't You Please Come Home • By The Light Of The Silvery Moon • Fascination • Give My Regards To Broadway • Mary's A Grand Old Name • Meet Me In St. Louis • Shine On Harvest Moon • Sweet Adeline • Take Me Out to the Ball Game • Waltzing Matilda • The Yankee Doodle Boy • You're A Grand Old Flag • and more.
_____00311656 ....$12.95

Songs Of The 1910s
Over 50 classics, including: After You've Gone • Alexander's Ragtime Band • Danny Boy • (Back Home Again) In Indiana • Let Me Call You Sweetheart • My Melancholy Baby • 'Neath The Southern Moon • Oh, You Beautiful Doll • Rock-A-Bye Your Baby With A Dixie Melody • When Irish Eyes Are Smiling • You Made Me Love You • and more.
_____00311657 ....$12.95

Songs Of The 20's
58 songs, featuring: Ain't Misbehavin' • April Showers • Baby Face • California Here I Come • Five Foot Two, Eyes Of Blue • I Can't Give You Anything But Love • Manhattan • Stardust • The Varsity Drag • Who's Sorry Now.
_____00361122 ....$14.95

Songs Of The 30's
61 songs, featuring: All Of Me • The Continental • I Can't Get Started • I'm Getting Sentimental Over You • In The Mood • The Lady Is A Tramp • Love Letters In The Sand • My Funny Valentine • Smoke Gets In Your Eyes • What A Diff'rence A Day Made.
_____00361123 ....$14.95

Songs Of The 40's
61 songs, featuring: Come Rain Or Come Shine • God Bless The Child • How High The Moon • The Last Time I Saw Paris • Moonlight In Vermont • A Nightingale Sang In Berkeley Square • A String Of Pearls • Swinging On A Star • Tuxedo Junction • You'll Never Walk Alone.
_____00361124 ....$14.95

Songs Of The 50's
59 songs, featuring: Blue Suede Shoes • Blue Velvet • Here's That Rainy Day • Love Me Tender • Misty • Rock Around The Clock • Satin Doll • Tammy • Three Coins In The Fountain • Young At Heart.
_____00361125 ....$14.95

Songs Of The 60's
60 songs, featuring: By The Time I Get To Phoenix • California Dreamin' • Can't Help Falling In Love • Downtown • Green Green Grass Of Home • Happy Together • I Want To Hold Your Hand • Love Is Blue • More • Strangers In The Night.
_____00361126 ....$14.95

Songs Of The 70's
More than 45 songs including: Don't Cry For Me Argentina • Feelings • The First Time Ever I Saw Your Face • How Deep Is Your Love • Imagine • Let It Be • Me And Bobby McGee • Piano Man • Reunited • Send In The Clowns • Sometimes When We Touch • Tomorrow • You Don't Bring Me Flowers • You Needed Me.
_____00361127 ....$14.95

Songs Of The 80's
Over 40 of this decade's biggest hits, including: Candle In The Wind • Don't Worry, Be Happy • Ebony And Ivory • Endless Love • Every Breath You Take • Flashdance... What A Feeling • Islands In The Stream • Kokomo • Memory • Sailing • Somewhere Out There • We Built This City • What's Love Got To Do With It • With Or Without You.
_____00490275 ....$14.95

MORE SONGS OF THE DECADE SERIES

Due to popular demand, we are pleased to present these new collections with even more great songs from the 1920s through 1980s. Each book features piano/vocal/guitar arrangements. Perfect for practicing musicians, educators, collectors, and music hobbyists.

More Songs Of The '20s
Over 50 songs, including: Ain't We Got Fun? • All By Myself • Bill • Carolina In The Morning • Fascinating Rhythm • The Hawaiian Wedding Song • I Want To Be Bad • I'm Just Wild About Harry • Malagueña • Nobody Knows You When You're Down And Out • Someone To Watch Over Me • Yes, Sir, That's My Baby • and more.
_____00311647 ....$14.95

More Songs of the '30s
Over 50 songs, including: All The Things You Are • Begin The Beguine • A Fine Romance • I Only Have Eyes For You • In A Sentimental Mood • Just A Gigolo • Let's Call The Whole Thing Off • The Most Beautiful Girl In The World • Mad Dogs And Englishmen • Stompin' At The Savoy • Stormy Weather • Thanks For The Memory • The Very Thought Of You • and more.
_____00311648 ....$14.95

More Songs Of The '40s
Over 60 songs, including: Bali Ha'i • Be Careful, It's My Heart • A Dream Is A Wish Your Heart Makes • Five Guys Named Moe • Is You Is, Or Is You Ain't (Ma' Baby) • The Last Time I Saw Paris • Old Devil Moon • San Antonio Rose • Some Enchanted Evening • Steppin' Out With My Baby • Take The "A" Train • Too Darn Hot • Zip-A-Dee-Doo-Dah • and more.
_____00311649 ....$14.95

More Songs Of The '50s
Over 50 songs, including: All Of You • Blueberry Hill • Chanson D'Amour • Charlie Brown • Do-Re-Mi • Hey, Good Lookin' • Hound Dog • I Could Have Danced All Night • Love And Marriage • Mack The Knife • Mona Lisa • My Favorite Things • Sixteen Tons • (Let Me Be Your) Teddy Bear • That's Amore • Yakety Yak • and more.
_____00311650 ....$14.95

More Songs Of The '60s
Over 60 songs, including: Alfie • Baby Elephant Walk • Bonanza • Born To Be Wild • Eleanor Rigby • The Impossible Dream • Leaving On A Jet Plane • Moon River • Raindrops Keep Fallin' On My Head • Ruby, Don't Take Your Love To Town • Seasons In The Sun • Sweet Caroline • Tell Laura I Love Her • A Time For Us • What The World Needs Now • Wooly Bully • and more.
_____00311651 ....$14.95

More Songs Of The '70s
Over 50 songs, including: Afternoon Delight • All By Myself • American Pie • Billy, Don't Be A Hero • The Candy Man • Happy Days • I Shot The Sheriff • Long Cool Woman (In A Black Dress) • Maggie May • On Broadway • She Believes In Me • She's Always A Woman • Spiders And Snakes • Star Wars • Taxi • You've Got A Friend • and more.
_____00311652 ....$14.95

More Songs Of The '80s
Over 50 songs, including: Addicted To Love • Almost Paradise • Axel F • Call Me • Don't Know Much • Even The Nights Are Better • Footloose • Funkytown • Girls Just Want To Have Fun • The Heat Is On • Karma Chameleon • Longer • Straight Up • Take My Breath Away • Tell Her About It • We're In This Love Together • and more.
_____00311653 ....$14.95

FOR MORE INFORMATION, SEE YOUR LOCAL MUSIC DEALER, OR WRITE TO:

HAL•LEONARD

7777 W. BLUEMOUND RD. P.O. BOX 13819 MILWAUKEE, WI 53213

Prices, availability & contents subject to change without notice.